THE TUNING FORK HEALING METHOD™

A Complete Guide to Clearing the Aura, Rewiring Identity & Upgrading Your Biofield

THE TUNING FORK HEALING METHOD™

A Complete Guide to Clearing the Aura, Rewiring Identity & Upgrading Your Biofield

By Elasa Tina-Marie Tiernan

Founder of R3 Miracles Healing Center

Creator of The Higher Self Method™ & The One-Code Model™

Master Teacher of Quantum Identity & Biofield Healing

R3Miracles.com • AkashicSoulPro.com

THE TUNING FORK HEALING METHOD™

A Complete Guide to Clearing the Aura, Rewiring Identity & Upgrading Your Biofield

Published by R3 Miracles Ministries Trust

Palm Harbor, Florida, USA

ISBN (Paperback): 979-8-9936562-5-0

Editing, Interior Layout & Design: R3 Miracles Publishing House

Cover Design: Elasa Tiernan & The R3 Miracles Creative Team

For inquiries, session bookings, or certification training, please visit:

R3Miracles.com • AkashicSoulPro.com

Contact: elasatiernan@gmail.com

Printed in the United States of America

TABLE OF CONTENTS

SECTION I — FINAL BLENDED TEACHING EDITION

The Science, Soul, and Structure of Your Human Biofield

Chapter 1: Understanding the Human Biofield

Before we begin tuning forks, muscle testing, or hands-on clearing techniques in class, we need to understand what we're working with. Your biofield is not new-age fluff or metaphor. It's a real electromagnetic field that organizes your physical health, emotional memory, personality structure, intuition, and your connection with your Higher Self.

This chapter is designed to teach, clarify, and demystify.

I want you—and your clients—to understand why you feel what you feel, why certain patterns repeat, and why sound and intention work so instantly when applied to the field.

This is a workbook, but it's also an initiation into understanding your energy architecture.

Your Biofield: The Electromagnetic Story of You

Every cell in your body produces electricity. Your heart generates the strongest magnetic field of any organ. Together, they create a spiraling toroidal aura—an electromagnetic bubble—around your body.

This field is:

- Measurable
- Intelligent
- Reactive
- Organizing
- Emotional

- Ancestral
- Interactive with your environment
- And deeply connected to your soul's blueprint

NIH calls it "the complex organizing energy field of the body."

That's exactly what it is—a living map of your physical, emotional, and spiritual experience.

Your aura isn't a random glow; it's a structured system that processes information constantly.

Your Aura Contains Your Timeline

This is where most people finally understand why their lives feel the way they do.

The biofield holds a chronological map of your experiences. Distances in the field correspond to chapters of your life:

- 6 feet out – conception, prenatal energy, birth imprints
- 3 feet out – childhood through adolescence
- 1–2 feet out – recent life experiences
- Skin level – present moment, current identity patterns

This makes tuning forks incredibly effective. You're not "guessing." You are literally sweeping through sound-coded memories suspended in the field.

When a tuning fork hits a distortion, you hear a change in tone. You feel resistance in your hand. The vibration behaves differently because it has found information.

Why Emotional Energy Stays in the Field

Emotions are electrical.

Thoughts are electrical.

Beliefs create electromagnetic impressions.

When something happens that your mind cannot fully process—a shock, betrayal, sudden stress, an emotional overwhelm—your system often cannot resolve the energy in that moment. Instead, it suspends it in the field.

This creates:

- Static
- Density
- Turbulence
- Pulls or magnetic "stickiness"
- Distortion
- Wave loops
- Charge pockets

These unresolved pockets remain until they are brought back into coherence, felt, understood, or reorganized through sound.

This is why clearing the field changes your mind, changes your identity, and changes your reality.

The Biofield Perceives Before the Brain

One of the most powerful teachings for beginners and practitioners alike:

Your field is your first nervous system.

Before your conscious mind can name an emotion or decide how you feel, your biofield has already sensed it, evaluated it, and reacted to it. This explains:

- Why you know something is "off" before you have a reason
- Why two people can enter a room and you feel them instantly

- Why trauma loops repeat even when you logically “know better”
- Why manifestation can feel blocked
- Why people drain you or energize you instantly

Your biofield is always reading the room, reading reality, and reading YOU.

Higher Self Guidance Lives in the Field

Your Higher Self communicates through:

- Expansion
- Intuitive clarity
- Inner knowing
- Sudden guidance
- Emotional resonance
- Directional “pulls”

When the field is congested with unresolved charge, these signals become muted. When it is clear, the connection is undeniable.

This workbook blends the Higher Self Method with biofield science so you can clear distortion, strengthen intuition, and embody the version of you who is already living your highest timeline.

The Biofield and Environmental Energies

Because your aura is electromagnetic, it interacts with:

- EMFs
- Wi-Fi and 5G

- Planetary shifts
- Collective fields
- Other people's emotions
- Sound and intention
- Belief systems
- Trauma patterns
- Identity structures

Belief plays a massive role here. If you believe you are fragile, your field contracts. If you believe you are sovereign, your field stabilizes.

And regardless of belief, cleansing your field simply feels better. It's energetic hygiene.

Why Tuning Forks Work

Sound is the perfect tool for reorganizing the field because sound creates coherence. The pure frequency of a tuning fork interacts with the disordered frequencies of emotional charge. Coherent sound gently harmonizes the distortion.

When a practitioner moves the fork through the field:

- They find the distortion
- The tone changes
- The fork begins to vibrate differently
- The practitioner can feel density through the stem
- The sound helps "comb" the charge toward the midline
- The emotional memory is digested
- The field restores its original blueprint

This is physics. It's wave interaction. It's resonance.

And it's one of the most effective energy healing tools available.

How Biofield Work Changes Identity

Identity is not just psychological. It's vibrational.

Every belief you hold about yourself—your worth, your safety, your capability, your potential—has a frequency signature in the field.

When the field changes:

- Subconscious patterns shift
- Emotional triggers dissolve
- Old storylines lose charge
- Generational wounds clear
- Higher Self embodiment becomes natural
- Manifestation accelerates
- Quantum leaps stabilize

This is why the Biofield Workbook integrates the One Code Method, the Higher Self Method, and sound science. Together, they create rapid identity transformation at the root.

SECTION II — THE AURIC TORUS & YOUR PERSONAL TIMELINE

Where Your Memories Live, How Energy Gets Stored, and Why Tuning Forks Can Find It

---

Chapter 2: The 6-Foot Toroidal Aura & Timeline Mapping

The human biofield isn't a vague cloud of energy that randomly floats around the body. It has structure, direction, and a predictable organization. The moment you understand the basic geometry of your field, everything else about energy healing suddenly makes sense.

The aura forms a toroidal field—a donut-shaped flow of energy that circulates from the head down through the body, out around the sides, and cycles back up. This torus shape is found everywhere in nature: in magnetic fields, galaxies, whirlpools, plasma rings, and the human heart. Your body follows the same electromagnetic architecture.

But what makes the human torus unique is this:

> Your aura is a spatial memory map. Your life is stored in layers.

This is the key to biofield tuning, energy clearing, intuitive scanning, trauma release, and Higher Self integration. You are surrounded by the stored frequencies of everything you've ever experienced—until it is cleared, resolved, or reorganized.

Let's break down the structure of your field so you can begin to read it.

The Midline: The Central Column of Your Life Force

Every toroidal field needs a center point.

In your body, that is the midline—a channel of energy running from the crown of your head down to the base of your spine.

Everything in the aura rotates around this central axis.

- It is the organizing structure of your energy.

- It is the highway for your Higher Self intelligence.
- It is the anchor point for sound clearing and tuning fork combing.
- It is the vertical channel that practitioners "pull" energy into during biofield sessions.

When emotional charge is brought toward the midline, the body can finally digest it. This is the same process your nervous system uses when you process an emotion internally.

The midline is the place of integration.

The Six-Foot Aura: A Living, Intelligent Field

Your aura typically extends about three feet in every direction—front, back, left, right—creating a six-foot diameter torus. Some people naturally expand farther; others retract their field tightly around the body due to fear, trauma, or chronic stress.

The field is alive. It expands and contracts in real time based on:

- Emotional state
- Stress level
- Environment
- People nearby
- Spiritual practice
- Nervous system regulation
- Identity patterns
- Belief systems
- Degree of trauma processing
- Connection with the Higher Self

A coherent, regulated person has a large, stable, even field.

An overwhelmed person has an erratic, collapsed, or patchy field.

This book and class help you bring your field back into coherence.

Your Aura Is a Timeline

Here is one of the most important truths you will learn as a practitioner or student:

> Your aura is not symbolic. It is chronological.

Different distances from the body correspond to different chapters of your life.

Outer Field — 6 Feet Out

This is the boundary of your aura.

It contains:

- Preconception energy
- Womb experiences
- Birth imprinting
- Early ancestral transmission
- Your first emotional programming

Many of your core beliefs about safety, belonging, love, and worth begin here.

Midfield — Around 3 Feet Out

This zone stores:

- Ages 4–12
- Childhood conditioning
- Family patterns
- Social imprints

- Identity formation
- First friendships, early school experiences
- Emotional mapping of the world

Nearly every One Code foundational wound lives somewhere in this midfield layer.

Inner Field — 1–2 Feet from the Body

This is where:

- Teenage years
- Early adulthood
- First relationships
- Financial imprints
- Body image beliefs
- Power dynamics
- Emotional trauma
- Repetition cycles

are stored.

Skin-Level — Present Self

This is the layer that directly interacts with your:

- Nervous system
- Emotions
- Inner dialogue
- Identity

- Decision-making
- Habits

When sound clears the outer layers, your current identity shifts effortlessly.

Left/Right Field Mapping: Masculine & Feminine Signatures

Your aura is not only chronological; it is polarized.

Right Side of the Body

- Controlled by the left brain
- Masculine in nature
- Logic, discipline, responsibility, protection, survival
- Often stores father-line patterns or masculine authority wounds

Left Side of the Body

- Controlled by the right brain
- Feminine in nature
- Creativity, intuition, emotional sensitivity, receptivity
- Often stores mother-line patterns or relational wounds

This polarity cross-over is critical when reading energy. A block on the left side of the field is rarely random—it often whispers something about a maternal wound or a feminine imbalance. And the opposite is true on the right.

Why Timeline Mapping Matters for Healing

When you can identify where a distortion lives in the field, you automatically gain clues about:

- What age it occurred
- Who was involved
- What the emotional theme was
- What belief formed
- Whether it belongs to you or an ancestor
- Whether it has been repeating
- What identity it created
- What needs to be released or upgraded

This is why biofield work is so efficient. You don't spend years talking about a pattern. You go straight to the frequency where it's still alive.

How Tuning Forks Interact with the Timeline

When a practitioner moves a tuning fork through the field:

- It passes through each layer of stored memory
- When it hits a pocket of unresolved charge, the vibration changes
- The tone might become dull, sharp, flat, buzzing, sticky, or tense
- The practitioner can feel density or resistance through the stem
- The sound entrains that distortion toward coherence
- The emotional memory comes forward for digestion
- The field reorganizes and the nervous system finally resolves the event

This is why sound is not symbolic; it is informational.

You are reorganizing energy and memory simultaneously.

Understanding the Toroid Helps You Understand Yourself

When you truly grasp this mapping, you begin to understand:

- Why you react the way you do
- Why the same identity patterns repeat
- Why certain relationships feel familiar
- Why you manifest or block certain realities
- Why your body holds tension in specific areas
- Why tuning forks feel like "they know where to go"

Your biofield is not random.

It is the electromagnetic expression of your soul's journey, your conditioning, your ancestral inheritance, and your Higher Self potential.

When you learn to read the timeline, you learn to read yourself.

SECTION III — EMOTIONAL CHARGE & SUBTLE MEMORY

Why Energy Gets Stuck, How It Shows Up in the Aura, and How Sound Sets It Free

---

Chapter 3: Emotional Charge, Memory Pockets & Why Tuning Forks Reveal Them

When people first learn biofield work, they often ask a simple question:

"How can a tuning fork reveal emotional memories?"

The answer is both scientific and intuitive. Emotional charge leaves frequency imprints in the field. Those imprints disrupt the flow of the aura and create measurable distortions. When coherent sound enters that space, it meets the distortion head-on. The field responds. The fork responds. The practitioner responds.

You are not guessing your way through the aura — you are interacting with stored information.

To understand how this works, you must understand the nature of emotional energy and the physics of unresolved experience.

Emotions Are Electrical Events

Every emotion you feel triggers an electrical response in your nervous system.

Fear, grief, shock, joy, excitement — each one has its own frequency signature, wave pattern, and effect on the electromagnetic field.

When an emotion is fully processed, the body:

- feels it

- acknowledges it
- metabolizes the chemistry
- reorganizes the field
- returns to coherence

But when an emotion is too sudden, too overwhelming, or too confusing, the system protects you by suspending the charge in the aura. This is not avoidance — it is a survival response. The field says:

“I’ll hold this for you until you’re ready.”

This suspended energy becomes what we call a memory pocket.

What Is a Memory Pocket?

A memory pocket (or charge pocket) is a cluster of unresolved emotional frequency held in the field. It is literally a compressed wave pattern created at the moment of emotional overload.

A memory pocket may contain:

- the emotional shock itself
- the belief formed in that moment
- the identity conclusion that followed
- the physical response pattern
- the person, place, or event involved
- the protective behavior learned afterward
- the subconscious meaning you attached

These pockets behave like “frozen time.”

The moment remains active until the field returns it to coherence.

This is why clients often relive scenes, memories, or emotions during tuning fork sessions—even without hypnosis. The charge has simply been waiting for permission to dissolve.

How Memory Pockets Disrupt the Field

A pocket of unresolved charge behaves differently from the surrounding field. It has:

- different density
- different harmonic signature
- different electrical flow
- different magnetic pull
- different sound response

To the practitioner, it may feel:

- like sticky air
- like a tug or pull
- like resistance
- like a pressure zone
- like heat, sharpness, or a "thick" vibration

To the client, it may feel:

- emotionally triggering
- physically sensitive
- tight, fluttery, or heavy
- numb or disconnected

- suddenly vivid or meaningful

Memory pockets are not random — they correspond to the exact timeline, the exact side of the body, and the exact emotional signature of the original experience.

Why Tuning Forks Detect Distortion

When a tuning fork vibrates, it produces a coherent wave — a pure, stable frequency that moves through the field evenly unless it hits something disorganized.

When the fork encounters a memory pocket, several things happen simultaneously:

1. The sound changes.

You may hear:

- flatness
- hollowness
- buzzing
- wavering
- sharpness
- shortened resonance

The tone reveals the presence of stored information.

2. The practitioner feels it through the stem.

The fork may:

- vibrate differently
- feel heavier or lighter
- feel resistant or "sticky"

- lose clarity
- pulse irregularly

Your hand becomes a diagnostic instrument.

3. The field responds.

The area may:

- expand
- contract
- pulsate
- grow warmer or colder
- “wake up” energetically

The aura reacts because the fork’s coherence has entered a space where energy has been holding its breath.

4. The charge begins to soften.

The memory pocket starts to reorganize.

This is the moment the story, the emotion, or the understanding may surface.

Tuning forks do not force release; they invite coherence.

Why Sound Heals the Field

Sound works because of entrainment — the tendency of chaotic or disordered frequencies to synchronize with a stable, coherent wave.

This means:

- Coherence reorganizes chaos.

- Order harmonizes distortion.
- Stability dissolves emotional knots.
- Pure tone brings memory back into the nervous system for completion.

When the sound "pulls" the charge toward the midline, the body finally has access to the memory. At that moment, the nervous system can digest the emotional experience that was once too overwhelming to process.

This is the essence of trauma resolution:

Energy moves out of suspension and back into flow.

Memory Pockets and Identity

Every pocket of unresolved charge contains the seeds of an identity belief.

For example:

- A childhood moment of rejection may become

  "I'm not wanted."

- A moment of fear may become

  "It's not safe to express myself."

- A moment of helplessness may become

  "I always have to do everything alone."

- A moment of overwhelm may become

  "I don't know how to handle life."

These beliefs are not chosen; they are encoded.

The biofield holds that encoded belief until it is reorganized.

This is why tuning forks, Higher Self Method, and the One Code work together so powerfully.

You are not simply clearing energy — you are dissolving the identity architecture that formed around the emotional experience.

What Happens When Memory Pockets Clear

When the sound reorganizes the pocket, the field and the nervous system immediately shift. Clients often experience:

- a sudden sense of relief
- emotional release
- clarity about the event
- understanding of the belief formed
- a lightening or lifting sensation
- improved intuition
- restored energy flow
- an identity upgrade

Once the pocket dissolves, the timeline changes.

Your present identity changes.

Your emotional default changes.

Your manifestation and quantum abilities increase dramatically.

You literally become the version of yourself that no longer carries that frequency.

This Is Why Biofield Work "Works"

It resolves the root, not the symptom.

It reorganizes the field, not the story.

It dissolves the belief, not the behavior.

It frees the timeline, not just the mind.

This is the science — and the soul — of emotional clearing.

Sound reveals the memory.

Memory reveals the belief.

Belief reveals the identity.

Identity reveals the new timeline your Higher Self has been waiting for you to claim.

SECTION IV — FREQUENCY TOOLS & TUNING FORK TECHNOLOGY

Solfeggio • Weighted vs. Unweighted • The Physics of Pure Tone

---

Chapter 4: Choosing the Right Tuning Fork — Weighted, Unweighted & Frequency Families

Most people are intuitively drawn to tuning forks without understanding why. They simply feel good. They feel "correct." They feel like they reorganize something inside of you instantly. That sensation is real. Tuning forks produce coherent, mathematically stable frequency waves that interact directly with the electromagnetic field of the body and the aura.

Understanding the different types of tuning forks—and when to use them—will transform your accuracy as a practitioner and expand your client results exponentially.

In this chapter, we break down the major tuning forks used in biofield work and why each one matters.

Unweighted vs. Weighted Forks

Two primary types of tuning forks are used in energy work and bodywork:

UNWEIGHTED TUNING FORKS

Used in the aura, for emotional clearing, timeline work, and subtle field harmonization.

Unweighted forks have no weights on the ends of the prongs. When activated, they create a light, far-reaching tone that radiates outward and travels through the field like ripples on a pond.

Unweighted forks are ideal for:

- Scanning the biofield

- Detecting emotional charge pockets
- Finding timeline imprints
- Combing disrupted frequencies toward the midline
- Releasing old beliefs and identity patterns
- Auric repair and boundary strengthening
- Opening or clearing chakras through sound alone
- Clearing residual EMF static in the field
- Integrating Higher Self frequency

The tone of an unweighted fork reveals everything.

It will change the moment it encounters distortion. It becomes your diagnostic tool.

In your hands, an unweighted fork becomes a listening device, a coherence generator, and an instrument of identity restoration.

WEIGHTED TUNING FORKS

Used on the physical body for deep vibration, grounding, pain relief, and organ support.

Weighted forks have small circular weights attached to the prongs. These weights create a lower, stronger, more penetrating vibration that can be felt deeply when applied to the body.

Weighted forks are ideal for:

- Placing on acupuncture points
- Stimulating meridians
- Spinal alignment
- Joint relief

- Muscle relaxation
- Activating nitric oxide release
- Decreasing inflammation
- Releasing cellular memory
- Grounding the nervous system
- Physical integration after a biofield clearing

Weighted forks are perfect for the “body integration” part of a session—especially when a client has just released emotional or ancestral content.

If the field work clears the blueprint, weighted forks help the body catch up.

Major Frequency Families Used in Biofield Work

There are many frequency systems, but in our work, we emphasize three main categories:

1. Solfeggio Frequencies (classic spiritual set)
2. Foundational Body Frequencies (128 Hz, 136.1 Hz, 432 Hz)

Let’s break each one down.

---

1. The Solfeggio Frequencies

These are ancient tones used in spiritual traditions, now rediscovered and popularized for their harmonic effects. They are beautiful for emotional and spiritual integration.

Core Solfeggio Set & Their Purposes

- 396 Hz – releases guilt and fear
- 417 Hz – clears trauma, transmutation
- 528 Hz – DNA repair, miracles, transformation
- 639 Hz – harmonizes relationships
- 741 Hz – cleanses, detoxes, clears mental blocks
- 852 Hz – awakens intuition
- 963 Hz – pure consciousness, connection to Source

These forks work wonderfully in the aura because they communicate instructions through harmonic resonance. They are perfect for students using unweighted forks for personal practice.

---

2. Foundational Body Frequencies

These are the "must-have" forks for any practitioner—even if they don't have a full set.

128 Hz (Weighted or Unweighted)

The gold standard tuning fork for bodywork.

- Stimulates nitric oxide
- Promotes relaxation
- Clears stagnation
- Opens meridians
- Helps with physical pain
- Integrates emotional released stored in tissue

The weighted 128 is your anchor for grounding after intense field clearing.

136.1 Hz (The Om Fork)

A universal healing frequency.

- Resonates with Earth's rotation
- Opens the heart
- Calms the mind
- Aligns the body
- Perfect for beginning and ending sessions
- Great for clients who are anxious
- Excellent for beginners

432 Hz

The "natural harmony" frequency.

- Reduces stress
- Restores balance
- Creates emotional softness
- Clears the mental body
- Harmonizes the field after intense releases

Everyone should have at least one of these three frequencies in their tool kit.

How to Choose the Right Fork for Each Session

Practitioners often ask,

"How do I know which tuning fork to use?"

The answer is part science, part intuition, and part muscle testing.

Use unweighted forks when:

- You're scanning the aura
- You're working with emotions
- You're mapping the timeline
- The client needs clarity, release, or identity shifts
- You're focusing on Higher Self integration

Use weighted forks when:

- The client is overwhelmed
- Trauma was just released
- You want to ground or stabilize their system
- They have physical pain or tension
- You're integrating energy into the body
- You want to stimulate specific meridian points

Use Solfeggio when:

- The emotional tone is clear
- You're doing spiritual clearing

- You're aligning the chakras

Use 128 / 136.1 / 432 when:

- You need instant grounding
- You're balancing the session
- The client needs nervous system support

You'll soon discover that the field will tell you exactly what it needs.

Why Frequency Choice Matters: Each Sound Carries Instruction

This is the secret most sound healers don't know:

> You are not just creating sound; you are giving the biofield a new command.

Every fork says something different to the field.

- 528 Hz says: "Return to your original code."
- 741 Hz says: "Remove interference."
- 136.1 says: "Come into harmony with the Earth."
- The weighted 128 says: "Relax and release."

The field listens.

The nervous system responds.

Identity follows.

This chapter sets the foundation for the actual tuning techniques we will learn next.

SECTION V — SCANNING THE BIOFIELD & READING ENERGY

Tone Changes • Resistance • Density • Emotional Signatures • Body-Sway Intelligence

---

Chapter 5: How to Scan the Field — Listening, Feeling & Interpreting Energy

Most people think scanning the field is some mystical psychic gift.

It isn't. It is a learned sensitivity, a blend of perception, physics, and intuition. Anyone can learn it—especially when supported by tuning forks, muscle testing, and the structure of the aura we've mapped in previous chapters.

The moment you activate a tuning fork, you create a coherent frequency that interacts with any dissonance in the field. Your job is to listen, observe, and feel how the field responds.

Scanning the aura is an art, but it's also a science of vibration.

This chapter teaches you how to sense:

- tone changes
- resistance
- emotional signatures
- energetic density
- timeline imprints
- ancestral layers
- and when an area is "done"

By the end of this chapter, you'll understand how to navigate the biofield like a seasoned practitioner.

What It Means to "Scan the Field"

To scan is to gently move an activated tuning fork through the client's aura, from the outer field (6 ft out) to the skin. You are listening for changes in the sound and changes in the feeling of the space.

A coherent field feels smooth.

A congested field feels bumpy, sticky, or turbulent.

When you scan, imagine you are:

- moving through a library of memories
- sweeping through atmospheric pressure systems
- listening to the "weather" of their energy
- reading emotional topography
- gently following the story that wants to surface

Sound reveals the distortions — you simply follow the feedback.

The Four Primary Indicators of Distortion

There are four main ways the field "speaks" to you when scanning:

1. Tone Changes
2. Resistance / Magnetic Pull
3. Density / Pressure Differences

4. Emotional Signatures in Your Body

Let's break them down.

---

1. Tone Changes — The Fork Tells the Story

A tuning fork will always behave differently when it meets a memory pocket.

You may hear:

- a flat, dull tone
- buzzing or static
- a shortened resonance
- wavering pitch
- sharpness or instability
- a hollow "drop" in sound
- a sudden brightness (release beginning)

Tone changes are the most direct diagnostic tool.

When you hear the tone shift, you've found information.

TIP:

If you're unsure whether a tone change is significant, use body-sway muscle testing to ask:

- "Is there a pocket of emotional charge here?"
- "Is this a timeline imprint?"
- "Is this the area that needs work?"

Your body will answer instantly.

2. Resistance & Magnetic Pull — Feeling Through the Stem

As you move the fork through the field, you will sometimes feel:

- the fork slowing down
- your hand being "pulled"
- a sense of stickiness in the air
- a subtle magnetic drag
- a slight pressure or heaviness
- difficulty moving smoothly

This is not imagination — it is the physics of interacting electromagnetic fields.

Distortion = the field is denser

Memory = the field is charged

Ancestral layers = the field is sticky or slow

Trauma = the field may feel sharp or erratic

The stem becomes an extension of your nervous system.

If you feel the fork "catch" on something, trust it.

---

3. Density or Pressure Differences — Atmospheric Changes in the Aura

Sometimes the field feels like a change in weather:

- sudden heaviness

- cool or warm patches
- thick, fog-like sensations
- thin or collapsed areas
- vibrating or tingling edges
- pressure changes like altitude

Each density signature has meaning:

- Heavy → grief, suppression, emotional overload
- Sharp → fear, shock, sudden trauma
- Sticky → entanglement, past relationship attachment, cords
- Cold → dissociation, avoidance, frozen emotions
- Hot → anger, activation, stored conflict
- Hollow → abandonment, loss, or emptiness
- Dense & pulsing → ancestral imprint

Over time, you will learn your own language with these sensations.

---

4. Emotional Signatures — Your Body Speaks

You are not separate from the field you are scanning.

Your own body will "read" the information through empathic resonance.

You may feel:

- pressure in your chest
- a knot in the stomach

- tingling in your arms
- heaviness in your heart
- sadness rising
- irritation
- sudden warmth
- a mental image
- a word or memory that isn't yours
- intuitive knowing

These impressions are not your emotions — they are the field communicating through you.

You are reading energy through your own instrument: your body.

Practitioner Rule:

Always use body-sway muscle testing to confirm what you sense.

This keeps your intuition clean and prevents projection.

How to Scan Step-by-Step

Here is the exact scanning method you will use in class and with clients:

Step 1 — Activate the Fork

Tap on an activator or your palm (never against metal).

Hold the fork by the stem, not the prongs.

Step 2 — Begin 6 Feet Out

Start at the client's outer field—this is their earliest imprinting layer.

Step 3 — Move Slowly Toward the Body

You are listening for tone shifts and feeling for resistance.

Go at the pace of the field, not the pace of the mind.

Step 4 — Stop When a Distortion Appears

The moment something changes, pause.

You've found a pocket.

Use body sway to get clarity:

- "Is this emotional?"
- "Is this ancestral?"
- "What age is this?"
- "Is more information needed?"

Step 5 — Combing Technique

Move the fork repeatedly through the pocket toward the midline.

You are helping the field return this charge to the nervous system for digestion.

Step 6 — Continue Scanning the Rest of the Field

Work down one side, then the other.

Front and back if needed.

Step 7 — Close with a Final Sweep

Use a grounding fork (136.1, 432, or weighted 128) to integrate.

How You Know a Pocket Is Cleared

This is where beginners get confused.

A pocket is “done” when:

- the tone becomes bright, clear, stable
- the fork glides without resistance
- the emotional charge drops
- you feel a release in your body or theirs
- the area feels neutral or open
- the client breathes differently
- body-sway says “yes, this is complete”
- the fork no longer pulls toward the spot

The field is intelligent.

When the charge is done dissolving, the sound will tell you.

Emotional Signatures & Their Sonic Profiles

Here are some common emotional tones practitioners hear:

- Fear → sharp, thin, wavering
- Grief → low, dull, muffled
- Anger → hot, buzzing, fast-vibrating
- Shame → hollow, collapsing, muted
- Shock → sudden volume drop, sharp edges
- Anxiety → rapid, fluttering overtones

- Suppression → flat, heavy, resistant
- Confusion → uneven, wobbling tones
- Relief (release) → brightening, ringing, clear tone

This is the "language" of the field.

Your Intuition + The Fork + Muscle Testing = Precision

The most accurate practitioners use all three systems together:

1. The fork reveals the distortion.
2. Your intuition interprets the emotional tone.
3. Body sway confirms the information.

This creates extraordinary accuracy.

No guessing. No projection.

Just direct communication with the field.

SECTION VI — COMBING THE FIELD & CENTRAL CHANNEL INTEGRATION

How to Move Emotional Charge, Restore Coherence & Rebuild the Auric Blueprint

---

Chapter 6: The Combing Method — Pulling Energy Toward the Midline & Delivering It into the Chakras

Once you've located a pocket of energetic distortion in the field, your next task is to help the system reorganize it.

The tuning fork reveals the charge.

Combing moves it.

The midline digests it.

The chakras integrate it.

This is the moment where emotional healing, timeline correction, and identity upgrading truly happen.

The combing technique is not merely a physical motion. It is a language you're speaking to the biofield:

> "Come home.
> Gather yourself.
> Rejoin the central channel.
> Return to coherence."

When you strike the fork and begin combing the area, you are escorting unresolved emotional frequency toward the part of the energetic anatomy that knows exactly what to do with it.

Why We Comb the Field Toward the Midline

The midline is the human body's energetic digestive system.

- It is where life force flows most strongly.
- It is the vertical highway for your Higher Self intelligence.
- It is the part of your aura that knows how to metabolize emotional charge.
- It is the place where disorganized frequencies can reorganize into their original pattern.
- It is where memory becomes understanding and energy becomes neutrality.

When emotional charge is suspended in the field, it remains unresolved.

When it is brought into the midline through combing, the nervous system finally has access to process what it could not earlier.

This is why clients often feel:

- sudden emotional clarity
- spontaneous memories
- intuitive understanding
- warmth or tingling
- deep breath release
- a shift in identity

The midline is the truth-center of the energy body.

How to Perform the Combing Technique

You will use this technique all the time—in class, with clients, and in your own self-clearing practice.

Here is the complete step-by-step method.

Step 1 — Activate the Fork Clearly

Tap the fork on a rubber activator or soft surface. Do not hit metal.

Hold it by the stem, allowing the tone to ring fully.

Step 2 — Place the Fork at the Distortion Point

Where the tone changed or resistance was felt is your entry point.

Pause there.

Let the fork speak to the pocket.

Step 3 — Begin Pulling in Slow, Gentle Strokes Toward the Body

Move the fork horizontally toward the client's nearest chakra or the central midline.

Your motion should be:

- steady
- patient

- slow
- smooth
- responsive

Imagine you are using a toothbrush for the aura—debris, static, charge, and information are being moved toward the place where the body can handle it.

Important:

You are not "fixing" anything.

You are restoring flow.

Step 4 — Repeat Strokes as the Tone Gradually Changes

You will notice:

- each stroke sounds different
- the tone begins to brighten
- the resistance decreases
- the pocket feels lighter
- the field begins to harmonize

This is the charge reorganizing itself.

Step 5 — Move the Charge into the Chakra Closest to Its Horizontal Position

Each distortion is horizontally aligned with a specific energy center.

For example:

- Distortion near the ear → throat chakra
- Distortion near the ribs → solar plexus chakra
- Distortion near the pelvis → sacral or root chakra

As you comb:

- Aim toward the chakra
- Bring the charge right up to the edge of the body
- "Hand it off" to the chakra's vortex
- Allow the tone to shift as it integrates

The chakra pulls the reorganized energy inward like a vacuum.

Step 6 — Column the Energy Up the Midline

Once the chakra accepts the charge:

- Move the fork vertically up the spine
- Lift the tone toward the heart, throat, or crown (depending on the emotion)
- Help the energy rise into the Higher Self channel

This upward motion is called columning.

It directs the newly harmonized frequency into a coherent vertical alignment where:

- meaning is found
- identity updates occur
- intuition awakens
- the Higher Self stabilizes the transformation

Combing brings the charge home;

Columning elevates it.

How to Know the Charge Has Integrated

A pocket is considered "integrated" when:

- the tone becomes crystal-clear
- no drag or pull is felt through the stem
- the chakra vortex feels open and receptive
- the client exhales or softens visibly
- the emotional intensity decreases or disappears
- body-sway muscle testing gives a clean "yes, this is complete"
- the area feels peaceful, neutral, or warm

You will always know.

The field becomes quiet and even.

The sound becomes open and clean.

You feel a sense of "rightness" in your body.

What the Client May Experience During Combing

Different people respond in different ways. During this technique, clients may:

- see images

- remember forgotten events
- feel warmth or tingling
- feel emotions rise and pass
- get intuitive downloads
- feel lighter or clearer
- yawn, sigh, or stretch
- release tears
- feel spontaneous compassion toward past events

This is the body completing what it once had to pause.

Why Combing Creates Identity Shifts

Every memory pocket contains a belief.

When you dissolve the pocket:

- the belief dissolves
- the identity built on the belief dissolves
- the nervous system resets
- the client steps into a new version of self

This is why your work is more than sound healing.

You are reorganizing the frequency architecture of identity.

The combing method is one of the most direct ways to update subconscious programming because it changes the energetic structure that the subconscious was referencing.

When energy is returned to the midline, the system updates the story.

When the story updates, the identity updates.

When the identity updates, the timeline changes.

The Fork + The Field + The Midline = Emotional Completion

The fork reveals the story.

The combing moves it.

The midline integrates it.

The chakra digests it.

The Higher Self rewrites it.

The client becomes the new version of themselves.

That is the full pathway of transformation.

SECTION VII — ENERGETIC BOUNDARIES & AURIC PROTECTION

Auric Cilia • Boundary Tears • Emotional Leakage • Field Filters & Repair

---

Chapter 7: Protection, Boundaries & Auric Cilia — How the Field Filters Information

Every human being has an energetic boundary—a protective membrane—that surrounds the aura. This isn't symbolic. It is a real electromagnetic interface composed of fine filaments of energy that function the same way the tiny cilia hairs in your sinuses function: they filter what enters and alert your system when something is off.

In energetic anatomy, these are called auric cilia.

They are one of the most important (and most overlooked) parts of the biofield because they maintain:

- safety
- sovereignty
- intuitive clarity
- emotional regulation
- energetic autonomy
- psychic boundaries
- identity protection
- and the ability to navigate life without overwhelm

When these cilia are damaged, torn, collapsed, or overstimulated, a person feels "too open" or "too sensitive," like they absorb everything around them. They may feel:

- drained by people
- overwhelmed in crowds
- hyper-empathic to others' emotions
- easily thrown off by conflict
- energetically porous
- anxious without knowing why
- overstimulated by environments
- confused about what emotions belong to them vs. others

Boundary collapse is not a personality trait. It is a biofield injury.

This chapter explains why.

What Are Auric Cilia?

Auric cilia are tiny energetic receptors located on the outermost layer of the aura. They function just like biological cilia:

- detecting incoming information
- filtering emotional frequencies
- sensing danger or misalignment
- communicating with the nervous system
- maintaining the integrity of the field
- keeping out intrusive energies

- regulating the “porousness” of the aura

If the aura is a house, the auric cilia are:

- the security system
- the temperature sensors
- the filters
- the early-warning signs
- the boundary walls

When the cilia are strong, a person feels grounded, centered, and sovereign.

When they are weak, torn, or collapsed, a person feels exposed.

How Auric Cilia Become Damaged

Cilia damage is common and almost always connected to emotional history.

The most common causes include:

Unresolved trauma

When something overwhelming happens and the system cannot process it, the field contracts or tears.

Boundary violations

Growing up without safety or autonomy damages the boundaries of the field.

Caretaker roles

If a child had to attune to everyone else’s emotions before their own, their field becomes hyper-permeable.

People-pleasing patterns

Letting others override your emotional truth can weaken the outer field layers.

Chronic fear or anxiety

Long-term stress thins the auric membranes.

Psychic overstimulation

Highly intuitive individuals often "extend their field" too far without protection.

Energetic entanglement or codependency

Shared emotional systems create weakened personal boundaries.

Ancestral trauma

Energetic vulnerability can be inherited.

When cilia are damaged, the aura becomes:

- too open
- too absorbent
- too reactive
- too merged with others

This is why energetic sensitivity often feels like a curse instead of a gift.

What Boundary Tears Feel Like in the Field

When scanning the field, boundary tears often present as:

- thinning at the edges
- sudden coldness

- static interference
- lack of resistance
- “leaks” in the energy
- sharp or fluttery tones
- areas where the fork sounds “hollow”
- difficulty finding a tone at all
- rapid tone distortion at the outer perimeter

Clients with boundary tears may report:

- exhaustion after small interactions
- feeling “attacked” by other people’s emotions
- taking on energy that isn’t theirs
- confusion about their identity
- empathic overwhelm
- chronic avoidance of social situations
- fear of being seen or not seen

These symptoms are not personality flaws — they are boundary injuries in the biofield.

How to Strengthen Auric Boundaries through Sound

Sound is one of the most effective tools for repairing energetic cilia.

When a tuning fork is moved along the outer perimeter of the aura:

- the coherent vibration repairs the cilia
- static discharges
- tears begin to close
- the perimeter "fills in"
- the aura remembers its original shape
- boundaries restore naturally

You will learn this technique later in the workbook, but here is the concept:

> Combing the outer field with pure tone reseals the auric membrane.

It is like smoothing wrinkles out of a fabric or restoring the insulation around electrical wires.

Boundary Strengthening Through Command

Because the biofield responds to belief and instruction, verbal or mental commands also help restore boundaries.

Examples include:

- "I claim my sovereign field."
- "My aura is sealed and coherent."
- "All energy that is not mine now leaves my field."
- "My field is closed to interference."
- "Only energy aligned with my Higher Self may enter my sphere."

Used with sound, these commands create extremely powerful results.

Boundary Health & Higher Self Embodiment

A person cannot embody their Higher Self if their boundaries are collapsed.

Why?

- The Higher Self requires clarity.
- Identity work requires containment.
- Timeline shifting requires stability.
- Intuition requires clean reception.
- Manifestation requires energetic autonomy.

If the field is porous, energy leaks out before it can cohere.

When boundaries are restored:

- intuition amplifies
- emotions stabilize
- manifestation accelerates
- identity becomes clearer
- the nervous system relaxes
- the client feels "more like themselves"

Boundary repair is often the fastest path to personal transformation.

Signs of a Healthy, Coherent Boundary

A coherent auric boundary feels like:

- calm presence
- emotional neutrality
- inner steadiness
- relaxed alertness
- being "in yourself"
- clarity about what is yours and what is not
- strength without defensiveness
- openness without vulnerability
- intuitive clarity
- effortless authenticity

Healthy boundaries aren't walls.

They are clarity.

They allow you to be open and sovereign, intuitive and grounded, connected and whole.

How to Teach Clients to Strengthen Their Own Boundaries

This workbook will guide you through several techniques students and clients can use:

- breathwork
- visualization

- humming and toning
- crystalline light protection
- tuning forks at the auric perimeter
- body-sway muscle testing
- Higher Self invocation
- One Code identity reinforcement

A client with a coherent field can handle far more emotional, spiritual, and energetic information without getting overwhelmed.

Boundary strength is personal power.

Chapter 8: Self-Clearing Techniques — Cleansing, Rebuilding & Maintaining Your Biofield

Most people walk around inside an aura that has never been intentionally cleaned, strengthened, or reorganized. They shower their physical body daily, but the energy field—the emotional, magnetic, intuitive body—is left full of residue, old memories, stress, and other people's projections.

A clear biofield is not a luxury.

It's a form of energetic hygiene, nervous system maintenance, and identity protection.

And just like brushing your teeth, this must be done regularly.

The good news is that your field knows exactly how to reorganize itself. You simply need simple practices that activate its innate intelligence.

This chapter teaches you the core self-clearing techniques you can do anytime, anywhere—with or without tuning forks.

These practices:

- clear emotional residue
- help you release other people's energy
- strengthen your boundaries
- restore your sovereignty
- reconnect you to your Higher Self
- accelerate your manifestation
- and regulate your nervous system

Let's begin.

THE SIX PILLARS OF SELF-CLEARING

All effective self-clearing methods fall into six categories:

1. Breathwork
2. Sound (humming, toning, forks)
3. Visualization & intention
4. Self-touch & auric brushing
5. Command language
6. Higher Self invocation

When combined, these pillars create a complete, powerful, and rapid clearing process.

We will teach each one.

---

1. Breathwork — Clearing Through the Prana Pathways

Breath is the fastest way to move energy through the field.

Your lungs act like pumps for the aura, pushing electromagnetic waves outward and pulling clarity back in.

The Reset Breath

Use anytime you feel overwhelmed, anxious, or scattered.

1. Inhale through the nose for 4
2. Hold for 2
3. Exhale through the mouth for 6

4. Hold for 1
5. Repeat 6–10 cycles

This breath clears emotional static and begins to reseal the boundary layers.

The Higher Self Breath

Use before meditation or intuitive work.

1. Inhale and imagine golden light filling your body
2. Exhale and imagine that light expanding 3 ft around you
3. Repeat until you feel “larger” and more coherent

This strengthens your auric perimeter and increases coherence.

---

2. Sound — Humming, Toning & Personal Tuning Fork Work

You don’t need a full set of forks to clear your field.

Humming

Your vocal cords produce a natural energetic tuning fork.

Hum at a low, comfortable pitch while moving your hands around your body.

This creates internal vibrational coherence and relieves anxiety.

Toning

Choose a vowel sound (“Ah,” “Oh,” “Ee”) and sustain it while imagining your field reorganizing.

Using Your Own Fork

If you have a fork (528, 432, 136.1, or your Sylphidia set):

- Strike it gently
- Hold it 6 inches from your body
- Slowly sweep it from crown to feet
- Repeat 3–5 times
- Then sweep front, sides, and back

You're essentially "combing" the field around yourself.

---

3. Visualization — The Field Responds to Imagery

The biofield responds to intention as if it is an instruction set.

Visualization gives it direction.

The Light Shower

Imagine a waterfall of golden or white light washing through your aura, clearing:

- residue
- attachments
- cords
- emotional debris
- old frequencies

This practice is extremely effective after social interactions, arguments, or stressful events.

The Boundary Shell

Imagine a sphere or membrane around your body, shimmering with:

- gold
- white
- violet
- or iridescent light

This activates the auric cilia and strengthens the outer field.

---

4. Self-Touch & Auric Brushing

Your hands are electrical.

Your palms emit electromagnetic signals strong enough to affect energy fields.

Use your hands to:

Brush the Aura

- Sweep hands down your body
- Move from head to heart
- Heart to stomach
- Stomach to hips
- Down the legs

This activates energetic drainage points and resets the field.

Press the Midline

- Place one hand on the crown
- One hand on the sternum or solar plexus
- Breathe deeply

This anchors your energy back into your central channel.

---

5. Command Language — The Field Responds to Authority

Your biofield takes commands literally.

It organizes around language that is clear, direct, and aligned with your Higher Self.

Use any of these:

- "I release all energy that is not mine."
- "My field is sovereign and sealed."
- "I recall all parts of myself back into my center."
- "Anything that is not aligned with my highest timeline dissolves now."
- "My aura is coherent, whole, and complete."

You will feel the shift instantly.

---

6. Higher Self Invocation

This is one of the most powerful self-clearing tools.

Sit still, breathe deeply, and mentally say:

> "Higher Self, reorganize my field to match the version of me I am choosing to become."

Then pause.

Your field begins reorganizing immediately.

You may feel:

- warmth
- tingling
- expansion
- clarity
- emotional calm
- a sense of “coming home”

The Higher Self always brings coherence.

THE COMPLETE SELF-CLEARING PRACTICE (Daily Protocol)

Here is the full routine you can do in 2–5 minutes:

1. Breathe (30 seconds)

4–2–6 breath cycle.

2. Hum or tone (20–60 seconds)

Focus on the heart or solar plexus.

3. Brush the field (30 seconds)

Up and down the body.

4. Visualize the Light Shower (30 seconds)

Gold or white light.

5. Command your field (15–30 seconds)

Choose one of the command statements.

6. Invoke the Higher Self (15–30 seconds)

Ask for alignment and coherence.

This is your "energetic toothbrush."

Daily use keeps the field clear, healthy, and magnetic.

Why Self-Clearing Matters

A clear field:

- makes intuition accurate

- reduces emotional overwhelm
- stabilizes identity
- accelerates manifestation
- improves sleep
- increases confidence
- enhances decision-making
- boosts psychic perception
- strengthens sovereignty
- helps the body heal faster

Your life changes when your field changes.

Chapter 9: Advanced Practitioner Work — Using Muscle Testing, Tone Diagnostics & Akashic Questioning During Sessions

Everything up to this point has built your foundation. You now understand the biofield, tuning fork science, emotional charge, boundary repair, and self-clearing.

Chapter 9 is where you step into master-level facilitation—the ability to ask the field questions, receive accurate answers, and guide a client through a multi-dimensional healing experience.

A practitioner who understands sound alone can help a client.

A practitioner who understands sound + the subconscious + Higher Self intelligence can transform a client's entire identity.

This chapter teaches the integrative method that makes your approach so different, so effective, and so accurate.

The Three Pillars of Advanced Biofield Facilitation

Every advanced session is built upon three simultaneous communication channels:

1. The Body (through body-sway muscle testing)
2. The Field (through tone diagnostics and resistance)
3. The Consciousness (through Akashic-style questioning and Higher Self dialogue)

When these three channels converge, the information becomes undeniable.

You're no longer guessing—you're translating.

Let's dive into each one.

---

1. Body-Sway Muscle Testing — Direct Subconscious Communication

The body never lies.

Muscle testing is one of the fastest, cleanest, and most precise ways to receive "yes or no" answers from the subconscious.

In the context of biofield work, you use it to:

- confirm whether an area needs more combing
- determine the emotion in the pocket
- identify whether a belief is still active
- clarify which fork to use
- locate the age or timeline of the imprint
- determine when a pocket is fully cleared
- check whether the work needs to go ancestral, past-life, or inner-child
- validate intuitive hits
- guide the session with accuracy

How to Use Body-Sway Muscle Testing as a Practitioner

Stand with feet hip-width apart.

Ask the question internally.

Let your body respond.

- Forward sway = YES
- Backward sway = NO
- Side sway = not now / unclear / ask differently

This tool becomes your compass.

When in doubt, test.

When unclear, test.

When intuition speaks, test to confirm.

Questions You Can Ask While Holding the Tuning Fork

- “Is this emotional?”
- “Is this ancestral?”
- “Is this event from childhood?”
- “Is there more charge in this spot?”
- “Is this pocket fully cleared?”
- “Do I need a different fork?”
- “Is this belief still running the client’s identity?”
- “Is the chakra integration complete?”
- “Is this ready to move to the midline?”

This keeps your sessions clean, accurate, and non-projected.

---

2. Tone Diagnostics — Sound as a Language

By now you understand that tuning forks reveal:

- density
- distortion

- emotional charge
- timeline placement
- identity patterns
- ancestral residue
- spiritual blockage
- field collapse
- boundary tearing

In advanced sessions, you use tone diagnostics as a symbolic language.

The fork tells you the emotional weather of the client.

Common Tone Signatures in Advanced Work

- Static / buzzing → anxiety, overwhelm, conflict
- Hollow / empty tone → abandonment, dissociation
- Dull / flat → grief, depression, emotional suppression
- Sharp / piercing → shock, fear, hypervigilance
- Heavy vibration → ancestral burden, lineage patterns
- Fluttering overtones → confusion, indecision, identity split
- Sudden clarity → release, forgiveness, emotional completion

A great practitioner listens with the ears, the hand, and the whole body.

---

3. Akashic Questioning — The Truth Hidden Inside Each Pocket

Once you find an emotional pocket, the field often wants to communicate.

This is where you introduce Akashic-style questioning—simple, clear questions that unlock the deeper meaning behind the energy.

These questions are based on:

- curiosity
- pattern recognition
- compassionate inquiry
- Higher-Self alignment
- and your signature method of “Who / What / When / Where / Why.”

Akashic Questions You Can Ask:

WHO

- “Who is connected to this energy?”
- “Is this linked to a parent, a partner, a child, or an ancestor?”

WHAT

- “What emotion is stored here?”
- “What belief formed at this moment?”
- “What identity conclusion did this event create?”

WHEN

- “What age or timeline is this from?”

- “Is this pre-verbal, childhood, adolescent, adult, or past-life?”

WHERE

- “Where in the timeline is this stored?” (Use distance + muscle testing)
- “Where in the body is this mirrored?”

WHY

- “Why is this still active?”
- “Why did the client hold onto this pattern?”
- “Why is this coming up now?”

This is not therapy.

This is field interrogation.

The energy itself already knows the answer.

Your questions simply open the door.

How These Three Pillars Work Together

Let’s walk through a real example:

Step 1: The Fork Finds a Distortion

As you scan, you hear a dull tone five inches off the left shoulder.

Step 2: Body Testing Confirms

You ask internally:

“Is this emotional?” — Your body moves forward (yes).

“Is this childhood?” — Forward (yes).

"Is this maternal?" — Forward (yes).

Step 3: Akashic Questioning Reveals the Story

You gently ask:

"What happened around age 5 or 6 with my mother that made me feel unsafe or unseen?"

The client instantly remembers.

Or the emotion rises.

Or the fork reveals more depth as you comb.

Step 4: You Clear the Pocket

Using combing + columning.

Step 5: Body Testing Confirms Completion

"Is this integrated?" — Forward (yes).

This is mastery.

Using Muscle Testing to Choose the Correct Fork

Practitioners often wonder which frequency to choose.

Muscle testing removes all guesswork.

Ask:

- "Is 528 needed for repair?"
- "Is 417 needed for transmutation?"
- "Is 741 needed for clearing interference?"
- "Is a weighted fork needed for grounding?"

Your body will always answer.

This is why your method accelerates transformation—it uses decision-making that's aligned with the field, not the ego.

Checking Identity Shifts in Real Time

Once the pocket clears, test:

- "Has the belief dissolved?"
- "Has the emotional imprint released?"
- "Is the new identity ready to anchor?"

Identify the replacement identity:

- "What identity wants to come online now?"
- "What version of me do I become when this is cleared?"

Then speak a Higher Self command:

> "I accept the identity of the version of me who no longer carries this pattern."

The field locks it in instantly.

When to Ask the Higher Self to Step Forward

Use Higher Self queries when:

- the client is confused
- the timeline is unclear

- the emotion is big
- the information is symbolic
- you've reached a blind spot
- the client's ego is interfering
- you want a higher resolution answer

Simply ask:

> "Higher Self, show me the greater truth behind this pocket."

or

> "Higher Self, what is the upgrade this client is ready for?"

This revelation lands like truth—clean, direct, and simple.

Signs You've Reached the Core Issue

A core issue is different from a surface distortion.

You'll know because:

- the tone shifts radically
- the client breathes deeply or tears up
- heat or tingling moves through the spine
- your hand feels suddenly lighter
- you get intuitive clarity
- the field becomes quiet
- the emotion resolves completely

- body-sway says: “YES. This was the root.”

This is the signature moment practitioners live for.

It’s when the entire timeline jumps.

Master Practitioners Use All Three Systems Instantly

In your method:

- Sound reveals
- Muscle testing confirms
- Higher Self guides
- Akashic questioning interprets
- Combing clears
- Columning integrates
- The midline digests
- The chakras balance
- Identity shifts complete the cycle

This is why your sessions create quantum leaps.

Chapter 10: Aura Repair, Boundary Reconstruction & Field Reinforcement Techniques

Clearing a memory pocket is only half of the work.

Once emotional charge releases and identity shifts, the aura must be repaired, sealed, and reinforced so the client does not fall back into old energetic patterns.

Just like a physical wound needs bandaging, an energetic wound needs coherence and closure.

Otherwise:

- energy leaks
- emotional residue returns
- external influences can enter
- the client feels disoriented
- the identity shift doesn't "stick"

This chapter teaches you how to repair tears, close leaks, seal the perimeter, restore auric cilia, and reinforce the field so your client leaves stronger than they walked in.

Aura repair is the difference between a session that feels good for a day

and a session that transforms someone for years.

Why Aura Repair Is Necessary After Clearing Work

Whenever a client releases:

- grief
- trauma
- shock
- ancestral weight
- relational entanglement
- old programming
- identity patterns

the field softens.

This is beautiful—because it means the nervous system is downloading the new coherence.

But in the moments after release, the aura may also feel:

- open
- tender
- porous
- emotionally vulnerable
- energetically raw
- rearranging itself

This is not weakness.

This is the field rewriting itself.

Your role as practitioner is to help the field reorganize faster and stronger.

How Aura Damage Appears in the Field

You can detect structural issues through:

Tone changes

- rapid drop-off
- fluttering
- distorted harmonics

Resistance

- weak
- collapsed
- inconsistent

Field density

- thin edges
- cold patches
- “holes” where the fork doesn’t resonate

Visual or intuitive perception

- grey fog
- static
- thin membranes
- cracked or dented layers

Client symptoms

- fatigue
- emotional leaking
- feeling "off" or "disconnected"
- sudden sadness
- overwhelm
- irritability
- psychic sensitivity

Aura tears always correspond to unresolved emotional history.

The Five Types of Auric Damage

Every practitioner should learn to recognize these:

1. Tears

Caused by shock, betrayal, sudden trauma, or conflict.

2. Holes

Areas where energy identity collapsed—often from repeated childhood wound patterns.

3. Leaks

Energy flows outward uncontrollably; very common in empaths, caretakers, and codependents.

4. Weak Perimeter

Auric cilia thinned or damaged; leads to hypersensitivity to others.

5. Corded or Tethered Areas

Energetic entanglement from relationships, past lovers, parents, children, or authority figures.

Each type has a specific repair protocol.

The Three Phases of Aura Repair

All aura healing follows this sequence:

1. Stabilize the field
2. Reconstruct & reseal
3. Reinforce & strengthen

Let's break it down.

PHASE 1 — Stabilize the Field

This step brings the nervous system back into coherence so the aura can self-organize.

Use grounding frequencies

- Weighted 128 Hz
- 136.1 Hz (Om)
- 432 Hz

Move the fork:

- along the central channel
- down the spine
- from crown to root

- through the lower field

Invite presence with breath

Ask the client to inhale deeply and exhale slowly.

Breath stabilizes the torus.

Use body-sway muscle testing

To confirm:

- “Is the field stable enough for repair?”
- “Does the client need grounding first?”

Once stability is confirmed, begin reconstruction.

PHASE 2 — Reconstruct & Reseal the Aura

This is the main repair stage.

1. Perimeter Sweep

Use an unweighted fork to scan the outer edge of the aura.

Listen for:

- tears
- skips
- tone drop-outs
- uneven resonance

Wherever tone disappears, slow down.

2. Stitching the Tear

Use slow back-and-forth motions with the fork along the tear, like sewing fabric with sound.

Imagine (and intend):

> The membrane closing.
> The cilia regrowing.
> The field knitting itself whole.

Tone will brighten when closure begins.

3. Light-Net Reconstruction

Visualize a net of gold or white crystalline light forming across weak areas.

Invite the client to visualize it too.

4. Chakra Vortex Resealing

Sweep horizontally toward each chakra and let it "pull" the remaining loose energy inward.

This anchors the repair from the inside out.

5. Command the Field

Use language that reinforces coherence:

- "The field is sealed."
- "Boundaries restored."
- "All tears are closed now."
- "I reclaim all energy that belongs to me."

Sound + command = rapid reconstruction.

PHASE 3 — Reinforce & Strengthen the Field

Now the aura is ready for reinforcement.

1. Use a High-Coherence Frequency

Such as:

- 528 Hz
- 936 Hz
- Sylphidia crown tone
- 432 Hz

Sweep around the entire aura:

- front
- back
- sides
- overhead

This strengthens and thickens the field.

2. Invoke Higher Self Alignment

> "Higher Self, anchor my energy into the timeline of my highest self."

This locks the field into the upgraded identity.

3. Teach the Client a Daily Reinforcement Practice

A simple 1-minute technique:

- inhale

- imagine golden light expanding
- exhale
- visualize the membrane sealing

This helps the repair hold.

How You Know the Aura Is Fully Repaired

A repaired aura feels:

- warm
- solid
- round
- even
- buoyant
- clean
- spacious
- grounded
- sealed
- sovereign

Tone becomes bright.

Resistance disappears.

The field's curvature feels symmetrical.

Clients often say:

- “I feel like myself again.”
- “I feel stronger.”
- “I feel lighter.”
- “I feel protected.”
- “I feel clear.”

That is the signature of a successful reconstruction.

Advanced: Repairing Cords, Tethers & Entanglements

If you find an area that feels like:

- pull
- stickiness
- emotional entanglement
- relational charge
- psychic imprint
- looping connection

You are dealing with a cord.

The Cord Clearing Process

1. Identify whose energy is entangled
2. Comb the area slowly
3. Use a cutting or dissolving visualization
4. Ask body-sway: "Is the cord fully dissolved?"
5. Seal the spot with a high frequency
6. Reinforce the client's boundary

Important:

You do NOT "cut cords."

You restore sovereignty, which dissolves the entanglement.

Boundary Reconstruction After Trauma or Identity Shifts

After clearing One Code wounds or releasing long-held identity patterns:

- the field expands
- the perimeter thins
- the cilia grow back
- the client becomes more sensitive
- the new identity needs anchoring

This is when boundary work is crucial.

Use:

- 136.1 Hz
- 528 Hz
- Vocal toning
- Visualization
- Command language
- Higher Self invocation

Reinforce the perimeter until the identity shift feels stable.

This ensures the new timeline holds.

Chapter 11: Chakra Integration, Ascension Anatomy & Delivering Energy Into the Centers for Healing

Once emotional charge is combed toward the midline, the energy needs a place to land. This is where the chakras—the energy centers—become essential. They act as the body's information processors, frequency converters, and identity anchors.

Every unresolved experience gets stored somewhere in the field.

Every resolved experience must be delivered into a center so the body can transform it.

This chapter teaches how the centers work as:

- emotional processors
- identity stabilizers
- memory integrators
- spiritual gateways
- Higher Self receptors

...and how to deliver cleared energy into them with accuracy and mastery.

Why Chakra Integration Matters in Biofield Healing

The chakras are not spinning wheels floating in space. They are bio-energetic organs—electrical hubs along the spine that process emotional, psychological, and spiritual information.

When you clear a distortion from the aura but do not integrate it, the energy:

- floats

- dissipates
- leaks
- becomes confused
- re-enters the field
- or fails to anchor the new identity

Chakra integration ensures the healing:

- becomes embodied
- becomes stable
- becomes part of the client's new identity
- becomes part of their timeline
- becomes part of their nervous system
- becomes part of their Higher Self expression

A cleared field + balanced chakras = Ascension Anatomy operating properly.

Ascension Anatomy: The Vertical Channel

The chakras are aligned along the Sushumna Nadi, the central vertical channel of the body.

This channel:

- carries life force
- carries Higher Self intelligence
- conducts intuition
- distributes energy

- houses the identity architecture
- acts as your personal timeline pillar
- receives guidance from the Higher Self
- anchors the new belief systems

When you column energy up the midline (from Chapter 6), you are allowing the vertical channel to bring the upgraded frequency to each chakra.

This verticality is what allows quantum leaps, identity shifts, and timeline upgrades.

The Seven Primary Chakras & Their Integration Roles

Here is how each center processes reorganized emotional charge.

This is essential for practitioners who want to guide integration intentionally.

---

1. Root Chakra (Muladhara)

Location: Base of spine

Theme: Safety, survival, physical identity

When charge enters the Root, the client experiences:

- grounding
- stability
- presence
- embodied strength

- release of fear
- belonging returning

Used for integration when clearing:

- abandonment
- early childhood wounds
- trauma
- survival stress
- scarcity frequency

---

2. Sacral Chakra (Svadhisthana)

Location: Lower abdomen

Theme: Emotion, creativity, relationships, sexuality

Integration here supports:

- emotional flow
- forgiveness
- creative activation
- relational healing
- unblocking desire

Used for integration when clearing:

- shame
- intimacy wounds

- betrayal
- creative suppression
- codependency

---

3. Solar Plexus (Manipura)

Location: Upper abdomen

Theme: Power, will, self-esteem, autonomy

When energy enters this center:

- confidence increases
- personal power stabilizes
- willpower strengthens
- self-trust returns

Used when clearing:

- guilt
- disempowerment
- identity collapse
- people-pleasing
- lack of boundaries

---

4. Heart Chakra (Anahata)

Location: Center of chest

Theme: Love, compassion, unity, coherence

Integration into the Heart brings:

- emotional balance
- compassion
- connection
- forgiveness
- peace
- self-love

Used when clearing:

- grief
- heartbreak
- abandonment
- inner-child wounds

---

5. Throat Chakra (Vishuddha)

Location: Throat

Theme: Expression, truth, communication, authenticity

This center processes:

- suppressed truth
- communication trauma
- confidence in expression

- fear of judgment

Used when clearing:

- self-silencing
- fear of visibility
- speaking wounds
- identity repression

---

6. Third Eye Chakra (Ajna)

Location: Between brows

Theme: Intuition, clarity, higher perception

Integration into the Third Eye increases:

- intuitive clarity
- inner vision
- Higher Self communication
- insight

Used when clearing:

- confusion
- doubt
- self-deception
- psychic interference

---

7. Crown Chakra (Sahasrara)

Location: Top of head

Theme: Higher Self, divine intelligence, consciousness

Integration here produces:

- spiritual clarity
- expanded awareness
- timeline upgrades
- pure consciousness
- “knowing”

Used when clearing:

- existential fear
- identity dissolution
- spiritual trauma
- disconnection

How to Deliver Energy Into a Chakra

This is the exact step-by-step method practitioners will use.

Step 1 — Locate the Chakra Line Horizontally

Where the distortion was found determines the chakra it must enter.

Example:

- Distortion at shoulder height → Heart or Throat
- Distortion at lower abdomen → Sacral

Step 2 — Comb Toward the Vortex

Move the tuning fork toward the client's body until you reach the edge of the chakra's "pull."

You will feel:

- suction
- magnetism
- sudden tone clarity
- energetic intake

The chakra "drinks" the reorganized frequency.

Step 3 — Pause & Hold

Let the fork ring at the mouth of the chakra.

This allows:

- memory to integrate
- belief to upgrade
- identity to reorganize
- nervous system to digest
- emotional meaning to settle

Step 4 — Column Up the Midline

Once the chakra accepts the energy, lift the tone:

- up the spine
- up the central channel
- toward the heart, third eye, or crown (where intuition wants it)

This moves the newly integrated frequency into the Higher Self pathway.

Step 5 — Body-Sway Testing for Completion

Ask:

- “Is the integration complete?”
- “Does the chakra need more time?”
- “Is this part of the identity shift finished?”

When the body says yes → the chakra is complete.

Higher Self Integration — The Final Stage

Once the energy arrives at the crown or upper heart region, invite the Higher Self to seal the shift:

> "Higher Self, anchor this integrated energy into my highest timeline and identity."

Clients often feel:

- tingling in the crown
- warmth in the chest
- emotional clarity
- a feeling of "clicking into place"
- sudden inner silence
- a new sense of self

This is the Higher Self joining the healing.

How You Know a Chakra Has Fully Integrated the Charge

Look for:

- bright, clear tone
- warmth or tingling
- ease of breath
- emotional neutrality

- clarity of thought
- lightness in the body
- symmetrical energy on left/right
- stable body sway

When the chakra integrates, the identity locks into coherence.

This is the end of the healing cycle.

Chapter 12: Full Session Flow — The Complete Practitioner Protocol from Beginning to End

This chapter is the backbone of your method.

It brings all previous chapters together into a unified healing sequence that practitioners can use confidently—whether with clients, in your Saturday class, or in their own personal clearing practice.

You now have all the components:

- scanning
- tone diagnostics
- combing
- columning
- chakra integration
- aura repair
- boundary reconstruction
- identity upgrades
- Higher Self embodiment
- muscle testing
- the One Code framework
- command language
- emotional processing
- sealing and closure

Now we sequence them into one seamless, powerful session.

THE FULL SESSION OVERVIEW

A professional biofield session in your method has nine stages:

1. Intake & Identity Framing
2. Energetic Preparation & Grounding
3. Initial Scan of the Aura
4. Locating & Diagnosing Distortions
5. Clearing the Pocket (Combing → Columning)
6. Akashic Questioning & Identity Upgrade
7. Chakra Delivery & Integration
8. Aura Repair & Boundary Reconstruction
9. Closing, Sealing, and Higher Self Alignment

Let's walk through each stage with precision.

---

1. Intake & Identity Framing

Every session begins with identity awareness.

You ask the client:

- "What are you currently struggling with?"
- "What identity pattern keeps looping?"
- "Which emotion is most active in your life?"

- “Which One Code gateway feels activated?” (optional)
- “What version of yourself do you want to become after today?”

This frames the session and gives you:

- the emotional tone
- the energetic direction
- the identity target
- the Higher Self intention

Clients don’t want a “relaxing session.”

They want transformation.

This question anchors that.

---

2. Energetic Preparation & Grounding

You prepare your own field first.

You become the coherent tuning fork.

Your setup:

- Center yourself
- Ground into Earth
- Open your central channel
- Connect to your Higher Self
- Command your field:

> “I am a clear channel for truth, coherence, and healing.”

Now you prepare the client:

- Offer grounding breath
- Use 136.1 Hz or weighted 128 Hz
- Sweep down their spine
- Stabilize the lower chakras
- Ask body sway: “Is the field ready?”

This sets the frequency foundation.

---

3. Initial Scan of the Aura

Begin 3–6 feet from the body.

Scan:

- left side
- right side
- front
- back

Listen for:

- tone shifts
- resistance
- density
- emotional signatures
- timeline placement

Use muscle testing to confirm:

- “Is this the first pocket?”
- “Is this the priority?”

The field will always lead you to the exact place you need to begin.

---

4. Locating & Diagnosing the Distortion

Once you find a pocket:

Pause.

Breathe.

Hold the fork steady.

Use muscle testing to determine:

- what emotion lives here
- whether it’s childhood, lineage, or relational
- whether it’s tied to identity
- whether a specific person or memory is involved
- whether more information is needed

Ask Akashic questions:

- Who?
- What?
- When?
- Where?

- Why?

This reveals the emotional truth hidden inside the field.

---

5. Clearing the Pocket (Combing → Columning)

Begin combing the charge toward the midline.

- slow, steady strokes
- fork tones shift as it clears
- body-sway confirms progress

At the midline:

- deliver the charge into the chakra aligned with the pocket
- hold the fork until the tone stabilizes

Then begin columning:

- move energy up the central channel
- lift it toward the higher centers
- allow the nervous system to digest the new clarity

This is the main clearing phase.

---

6. Akashic Questioning & Identity Upgrade

As the pocket clears, the identity shift becomes available.

Ask:

- "What belief was formed here?"
- "What version of you died here?"
- "What version of you was born here?"
- "What identity do you choose now?"

Then anchor with command:

> "I now embody the identity of the version of me who no longer holds this pattern."

Use Higher Self invocation:

> "Higher Self, show the new timeline this client is stepping into."

This locks the new identity into the timeline.

---

7. Chakra Delivery & Integration

Deliver reorganized energy into the appropriate chakra.

Signs of integration:

- clarity
- warmth
- breath opening
- brighter tone
- client sighs or softens
- emotional neutrality

Column upward to:

- heart
- third eye
- or crown

Muscle test:

- “Is integration complete?”
- “Does more clearing need to happen here?”

This stage anchors emotional healing in the body.

---

8. Aura Repair & Boundary Reconstruction

Now seal and strengthen the field.

Use:

- perimeter sweeps
- auric stitching
- light-net reconstruction
- boundary commands
- 528 Hz, 432 Hz, or Sylphidia crown tone

Repair:

- tears
- leaks
- holes

- cilia damage
- relational cords

Command:

> "My aura is sealed. My boundaries are strong. My energy is sovereign."

This finalizes the session's transformation.

---

9. Closing, Sealing, and Higher Self Alignment

Close the session by:

- sweeping the entire aura with a coherent tone
- grounding through the feet
- checking with muscle testing: "Is the session complete?"
- anchoring the new identity with a Higher Self command

Final words spoken aloud (you can train your practitioners to use these):

> "Higher Self, anchor this version of me fully.
> Seal this work in coherence, truth, and alignment
> with my highest timeline."

Clients feel:

- whole
- clear
- centered

- lighter
- empowered
- protected
- embodied

This is the signature of REAL transformation.

THE MINI "POCKET SESSION" FLOW (For Quick 15-Min Clearings)

Sometimes practitioners need a shorter flow.

Here is your official mini-session:

1. Ground (136.1 or 128 Hz)
2. Scan
3. Locate distortion
4. Comb → Column
5. Chakra integrate
6. Repair perimeter
7. Close with a command

This simple flow still delivers powerful results.

Section 13

PRACTITIONER HYGIENE (Before & After Sessions)

This section trains your facilitators to stay clean, sovereign, and powerful.

BEFORE SESSION — Practitioner Prep

1. Seal Your Field

Say:

> "My aura is sealed. My field is sovereign."

2. Ground

Use:

- 136.1 Hz
- 128 Hz weighted
- or 3 deep belly breaths

3. Open the Central Channel

Visualize light running from crown → root → Earth.

4. Connect to Higher Self

Say:

> "I am a clear channel for truth, clarity, and coherence."

5. Set Boundaries

> "Nothing enters my field without my permission."

AFTER SESSION — Practitioner Clearing

1. Cut the Connection

Use intention or 528 Hz.

Say:

> "I release all energy that is not mine."

2. Shake Out the Hands & Arms

Moves energy down and out.

3. Sweep Your Own Aura

Front, sides, back.

4. Breath Reset

Exhale sharply three times.

5. Re-Anchor Your Identity

> "I return fully to myself. I am whole."

Section 14

SIMPLE CLIENT CLEARING TECHNIQUES (Take-Home Tools)

Give these as a printed page or add to the e-book as a self-care chapter.

---

1. Daily Light Shower (30 seconds)

Visualize golden light washing from head to feet, clearing residue.

2. Heart Humming (20–60 seconds)

Hum softly while hands are over the chest to stabilize emotion.

3. Boundary Sphere (10 seconds)

Imagine a 3-ft bubble of clean light around the body.

4. Command Language

Say once daily:

> "All energy that is not mine now leaves my field."

5. Breath Reset

Inhale 4 → hold 2 → exhale 6

Repeat 3–5 cycles.

6. Palm Sweeping Technique

Brush downward over head, chest, abdomen, legs to clear static.

7. Higher Self Invocation

> "Higher Self, reorganize my field to match my highest identity."

Section 15

GLOSSARY OF TERMS

A clean, professional glossary for your e-book or handouts:

Akashic Questioning

A method of intuitive inquiry using "Who, What, When, Where, Why" to reveal the emotional or identity origin of a field distortion.

Ascension Anatomy

The vertical alignment of chakras, central channel, nervous system, and Higher Self that allows identity upgrades and quantum timeline shifts.

Aura / Biofield

The electromagnetic field surrounding the body, containing emotional memory, identity patterns, and energetic timelines.

Auric Cilia

Fine energetic hairs on the outer edge of the aura that filter information, maintain boundaries, and sense energetic changes.

Boundary Reconstruction

Repairing tears, thinning, or holes in the auric membrane to restore protection and sovereignty.

Chakra Integration

Delivering reorganized emotional charge into the corresponding energy center for digestion and stabilization.

Central Channel (Sushumna)

The vertical energetic pathway inside the body where life force, Higher Self intelligence, and identity alignment flow.

Columning

Vertical movement of reorganized energy up the spine from lower chakras toward the higher centers.

Combing

Moving tuning fork vibrations toward the midline to gather and reorganize emotional charge stored in the aura.

Distortion / Memory Pocket

A density, tone change, or resistance in the aura created by unresolved emotional events.

EMF Debris

Energetic interference or static absorbed from external environments, technology, or emotional exchange.

Higher Self

Your expanded consciousness, outside of linear time, offering clarity, identity upgrades, and alignment with your highest timeline.

Identity Architecture

The internal frequency blueprint that determines how you think, behave, manifest, and respond emotionally.

One Code

Your foundational subconscious identity pattern that shapes your emotional wounds and life trajectory.

Perimeter Sweep

Running a tuning fork around the outer boundary of the aura to detect tears and repair cilia.

Practitioner Hygiene

Energetic preparation and clearing done before and after sessions to avoid taking on client energy.

Solfeggio Frequencies

Ancient harmonic tones used for spiritual, emotional, and energetic clearing.

Sylphidia Frequencies

High-precision tuning fork tones aligned to energy centers for advanced biofield work.

Tone Diagnostics

Reading the emotional or timeline information revealed through changes in tuning fork resonance.

Vertical Alignment

The process of connecting root to crown through breath, light, and intention for coherent energy flow.

SESSION NOTES — Practitioner Worksheet

Use this page during or after a session to track client progress and map the field.

Client Name:________________________________

Date:______________________________________

Primary Intention / Identity Goal:

____

____

Presenting Emotion or Pattern (One Code if applicable):

____

____

1. INITIAL SCAN FINDINGS

- Distortion locations: ______________________________
- Emotional tone: __________________________________
- Side / timeline correlation: __________________________
- Initial muscle test insights: __________________________

---

2. CLEARING WORK

Pocket Located At: ______________________________

Emotion(s) Found: _______________________________

Age / Timeline: _________________________________

Akashic Insights (Who/What/Why):

____

Technique Used (circle):

Combing • Columning • Chakra Delivery • Tone Shift • Breath • Command

3. CHAKRA INTEGRATION

Center Used: ______________________________

Signs of Integration: __________________________

4. AURA REPAIR & BOUNDARY WORK

Tears/Holes/Leaks Found: __________________________

Corrections Made: ______________________________

Final Tone: __________________________________

5. IDENTITY UPGRADE

Old Identity Belief Released:

New Identity Anchored:

6. CLOSING NOTES / HIGHER SELF MESSAGE

Body Sway Muscle Testing

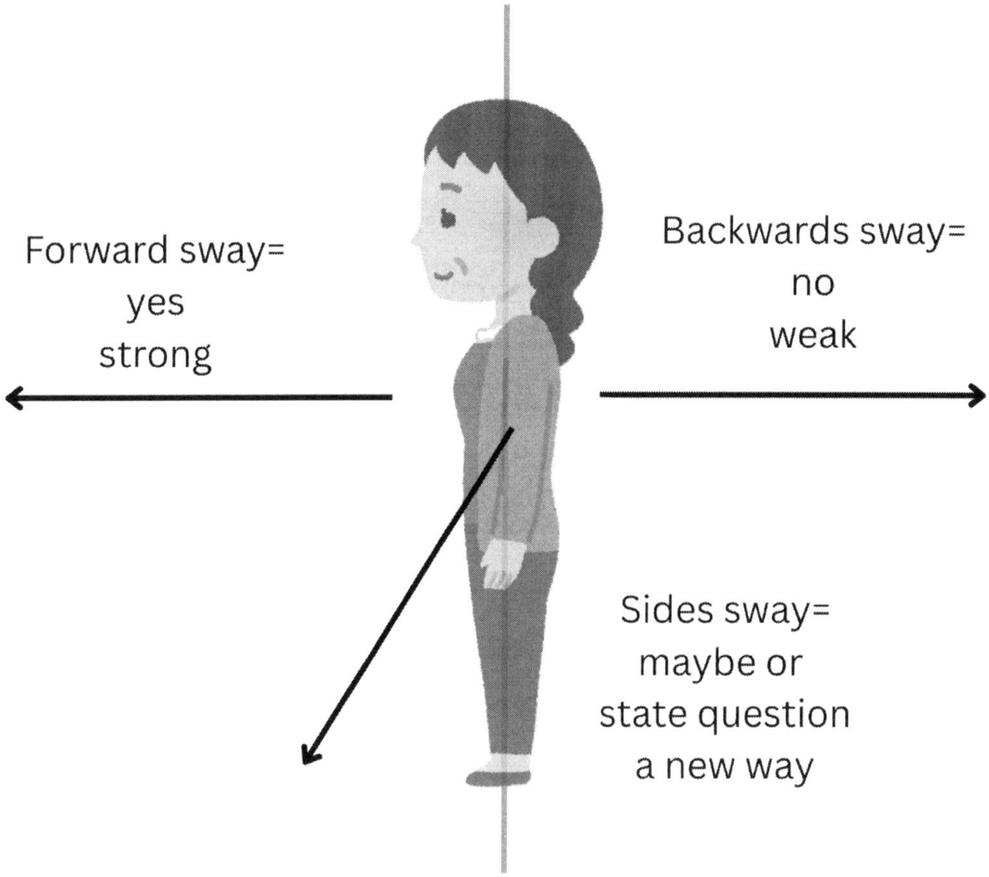

Anatomy of the biofield:

How to read the biofield

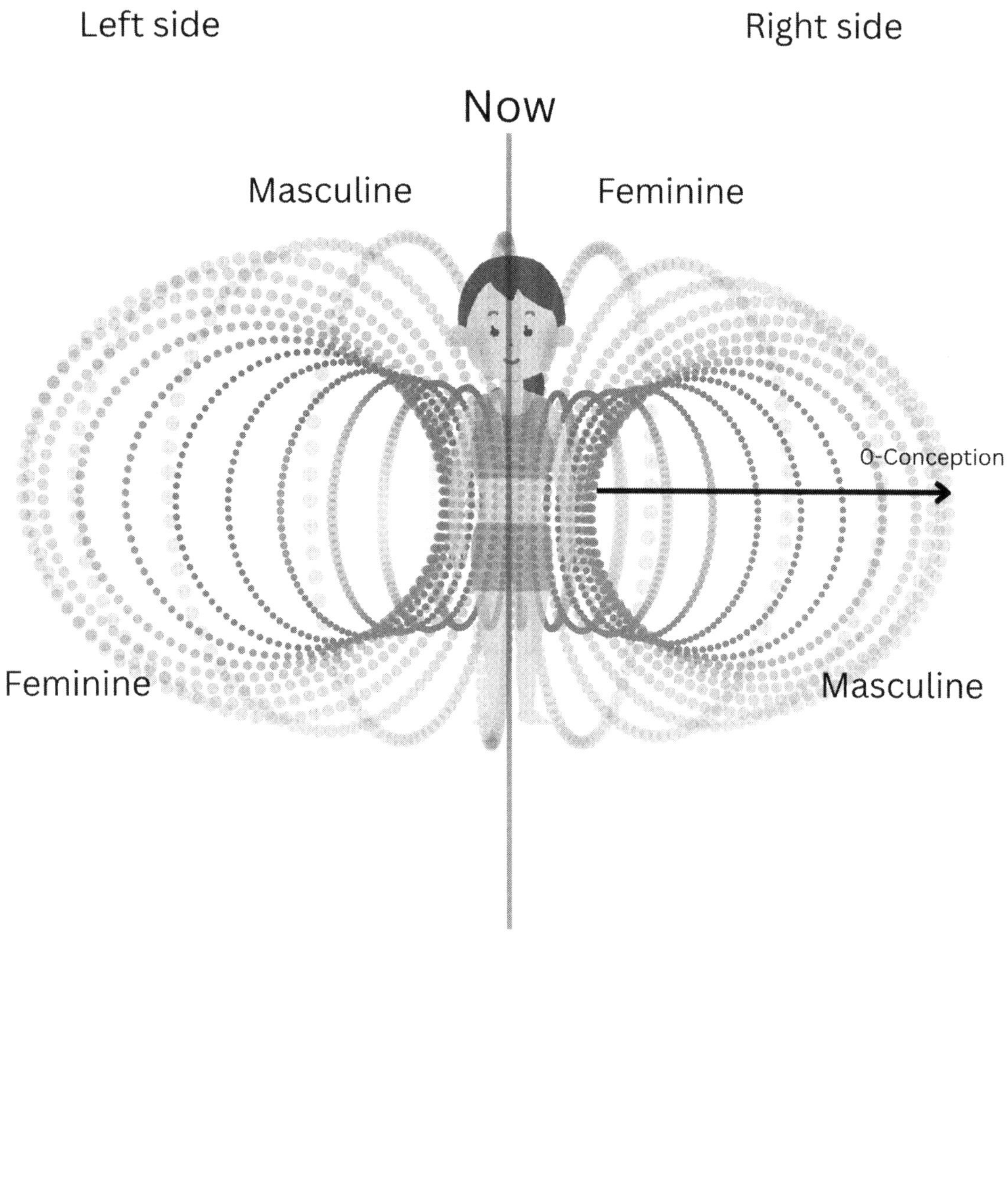

Comb towards closest energy center

and then column up the energy center

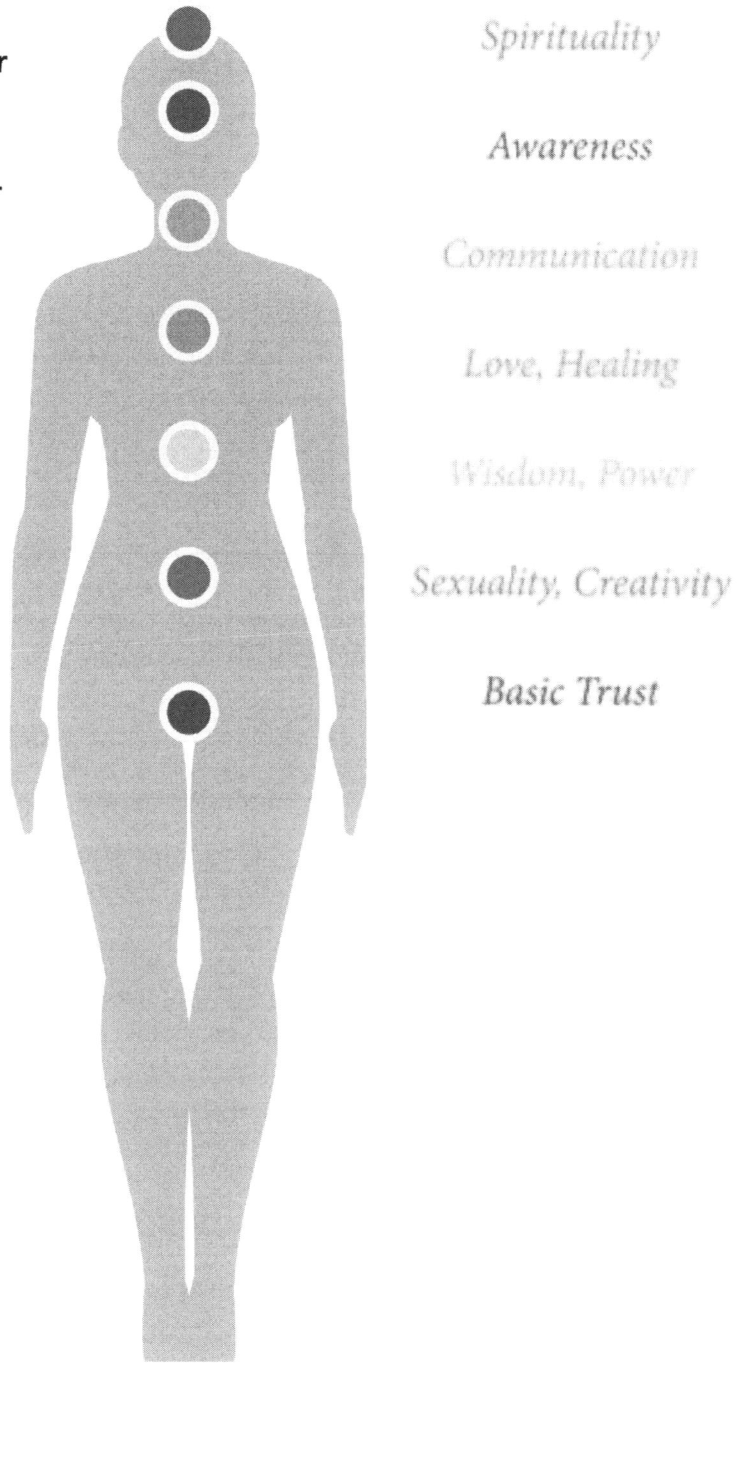

REFERENCES

Biofield Science & Electromagnetic Research

Ahn, A., et al. Biofield Science and Healing: History, Terminology, and Concepts. Global Advances in Health and Medicine, 2017.

Rubik, B. The Biofield Hypothesis: Its Biophysical Basis and Role in Medicine. Journal of Alternative and Complementary Medicine, 2002.

Oschman, J. Energy Medicine: The Scientific Basis. Elsevier Science, 2000.

McCraty, R., & Childre, D. Coherence: A New Scientific Foundation for Health and Performance. HeartMath Institute, 2010.

Sound Healing & Frequency Research

Maman, F. The Role of Music in Integrative Medicine. Tama-Do Academy, 2014.

Goldman, J. Healing Sounds: The Power of Harmonics. Inner Traditions, 2002.

Beaulieu, J. Human Tuning: Sound Healing with Tuning Forks. BioSonic Enterprises, 2010.

Tuning Forks & Biofield Methods

McKusick, E. Tuning the Human Biofield. Healing Arts Press, 2014.

McKusick, E. Electric Body, Electric Health. St. Martin's Essentials, 2021.

Biofield Tuning Institute. Explorations in Sound, Electricity & the Human Field.

Subconscious Repatterning, Identity & Psychology

Lipton, B. The Biology of Belief. Hay House, 2005.

Dispenza, J. Breaking the Habit of Being Yourself. Hay House, 2012.

Siegel, D. J. The Developing Mind. Guilford Press, 2012.

Quantum Consciousness & Higher Self Perspectives

Goddard, N. Feeling is the Secret. DeVorss Publications, 1944.

Cannon, D. The Convoluted Universe Series. Ozark Mountain Publishing.

Newton, M. Journey of Souls. Llewellyn, 1994.

Weiss, B. Many Lives, Many Masters. Simon & Schuster, 1988.

Energy Systems, Chakras & Esoteric Physiology

Judith, A. Eastern Body, Western Mind. Celestial Arts, 2004.

Leadbeater, C.W. The Chakras. Quest Books.

Sivananda, S. Kundalini Yoga. Divine Life Society.

Identity, Self-Concept & Transformation

Shinn, F.S. The Game of Life and How to Play It. 1925.

Goddard, N. The Power of Awareness. 1952.

Tolle, E. A New Earth. Penguin Books.

Works & Methods Created by Elasa Tina-Marie Tiernan

Tiernan, E. The Higher Self Method™. R3 Miracles.

Tiernan, E. The One-Code Model™. R3 Miracles.

Tiernan, E. Reality Alchemy™. R3 Miracles.

Tiernan, E. The Tuning Fork Healing Method™. R3 Miracles.

About the Author

Elasa Tina-Marie Tiernan

Master Energy Healer • Quantum Soul Mentor

Creator of The Tuning Fork Healing Method™, Higher Self Method™ & The One-Code Model™

Elasa Tina-Marie Tiernan has spent over twenty years guiding individuals and practitioners into deep emotional healing, Higher Self embodiment, and quantum identity transformation. She is the founder of R3 Miracles Healing Center in Palm Harbor, Florida, a multidimensional learning space offering advanced modalities such as tuning fork therapy, Higher Self regression, quantum soul work, identity rewiring, biofield balancing, and multidimensional coaching.

Elasa is the creator of several respected spiritual systems, including:

- The Tuning Fork Healing Method™
- The Higher Self Method™
- The One-Code Model™
- Reality Alchemy™
- Quantum Soul Practitioner Certification

Her teachings blend:

- biofield science
- emotional charge clearing
- sound-frequency diagnostics
- metaphysical identity reprogramming
- Akashic-style questioning
- Higher Self communication
- multidimensional timelines

- and practical embodiment strategies

She has facilitated thousands of sessions, regressions, workshops, and practitioner trainings for clients around the world. Her work is known for being clear, transformational, scientifically grounded, and energetically precise.

Elasa's mission is to empower individuals to reclaim their sovereign identity, heal their emotional imprints, embody their Highest Self, and activate the original divine blueprint encoded in their biofield.

She lives and teaches in Palm Harbor, Florida, where R3 Miracles serves as a sanctuary for deep healing, spiritual mastery, and community expansion.

Connect or learn more:

R3Miracles.com

AkashicSoulPro.com

Email: elasatiernan@gmail.com

Printed in Dunstable, United Kingdom

78015595R00075